Precious Goods:
From Salt to Silk

by Laura Johnson
and Joanna Korba

Scott Foresman
is an imprint of

Glenview, Illinois • Boston, Massachusetts • Chandler, Arizona
Upper Saddle River, New Jersey

Consider these common expressions used to describe a person's worth—or worthlessness: *Lee is the salt of the earth. Lee is worth his weight in gold. Lee is a diamond in the rough. Poor Lee! You can't make a silk purse out of a sow's ear.* What do these expressions have in common?

All involve goods—gold, diamonds, silk, and salt—that were precious **commodities** in ancient times. Diamonds and gold are still highly valued today. Silk, while it is still valued, is now a popular, relatively affordable fabric that many people are able to buy. Salt, however, can be found on everyone's table. You're probably surprised to see it included. While salt has ceased to be a precious commodity, something else has come along to take its place—oil.

What makes something a precious commodity? For one thing, it must be wanted. For another, it must be rare. Generally speaking, the more scarce something is, the more money it can bring. Buyers must desire the commodity badly enough to spend lots of money willingly to acquire it.

Over the years, the hot desert sun evaporated water in the salty Dead Sea, leaving behind huge salt deposits.

Salt, an Ancient Treasure

As you sprinkle some salt on your vegetables tonight, think about this: In ancient China, a spoonful of salt could be traded for an ounce of gold. In ancient Rome, salt was used as money. Roman citizens could pay their taxes with salt, and Roman soldiers were given salt as part of their pay. In fact, our word *salary* is derived from the Latin word for salt, *sal*. (Latin was the language of the ancient Romans.)

Salt is a harmless mineral formed from two potentially harmful elements: sodium and chlorine. Sodium is an unstable metal that can suddenly burst into flame. Chlorine is a deadly gas. When the two react, they form sodium chloride, or table salt.

The Value of Salt

In ancient times, the main way to **preserve** food was to salt it. There were no refrigerators to keep food from spoiling quickly. And ancient peoples didn't know how to can goods to keep the contents germ free.

Salt was also highly valued, and still is, as a seasoning. But it is more important to humans than that. Ancient peoples didn't know it, but salt, like water, is essential to the health of our cells. Without both water and salt, our cells would die—and so would we.

People needed and wanted salt. In addition, it was hard to obtain. Salt is found almost everywhere on Earth, but this was not known until the last century. Before then, salt was searched for and fought over.

There are two main sources of this popular mineral. Seawater contains about 3.5 percent salt. Ancient peoples got salt from the sea by pouring ocean water into huge basins that they left in the sun to evaporate. This process took a long time and could only be done in hot, sunny regions with easy access to saltwater.

Salt can also be found underground, in huge deposits that are the remains of prehistoric oceans buried millions of years ago. Getting this salt requires locating, **excavating**, and operating salt mines.

Trading in Salt

In early times, salted food was traded, since it was lighter and easier to handle than heavy bags of salt. Around 2800 B.C., the ancient Egyptians began trading salted fish to another ancient people, the Phoenicians, who had established trade cities all around the Mediterranean.

There was a wealth of salt to be gotten from another part of Africa. But there was a problem. The salt was in dried-out lake beds in the vast Sahara, the largest desert in the world. How could it be transported from deep in the scorching Sahara to various trade cities in West Africa?

The solution was to domesticate an animal that could survive intense heat and a lack of water: the camel. About a thousand years ago, traders began dealing directly in salt, traveling trade routes from the Saharan salt mines to the coast of the Mediterranean.

People and camels journeyed together in caravans. Once the caravan reached the coast, the salt was loaded onto ships sailing to European ports. Major cities, such as Genoa and Pisa in Italy and

Lisbon in Portugal, were centers of the salt trade. By the Middle Ages, caravans of as many as 40,000 camels laden with salt and other goods were making the long trek through the Sahara.

Deep-drilling technology, introduced in the early 1800s, provided easier access to underground salt deposits. And the need for salt as a preservative disappeared with advances in canning and refrigeration. What was once a precious commodity has now become a basic part of our everyday lives.

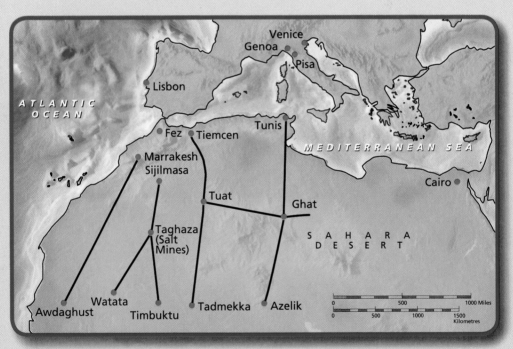

It took as long as six months for caravans from West Africa to reach the Mediterranean coast.

Silk, a Prized Secret

Silk is an elegant fabric from an inelegant source—a worm. The creature in question, known as a silkworm moth, is native to China. It lives its first 45 days as a worm, feeding on leaves (preferably from a mulberry tree). Once grown, it wraps itself in a sheath called a cocoon. Inside, the silkworm undergoes a dramatic change, emerging as a moth. During its brief adulthood (lasting only two or three days), the moth does not eat and rarely flies. It does mate though, and the female lays 300–500 eggs before dying.

The silkworm's cocoon consists of one continuous silken thread. It is this thread that is unraveled, twisted together into thicker strands of thread, and woven into silk cloth.

The silkworm spins its cocoon from a single silk thread that is about 1,000 yards long.

The Value of Silk

Silk is the strongest of all natural fibers. Silk cloth is light, cool, and smooth, with a fine **luster**. It takes dye well and can be produced in a variety of rich colors. The Chinese discovered how to turn silkworm cocoons into silk cloth almost 5,000 years ago. For hundreds of years, they fiercely guarded the source of their silk and their silk-making process.

About 3,000 years ago, the Chinese began trading silk cloth abroad. Not too long after, caravans were regularly carrying silk to India, Persia (now Iran), and elsewhere. Silk—so beautiful, so rare, and so secret— was in great demand.

For a thousand years more, the Chinese were able to keep their secret. By the second century A.D., though, India was producing and shipping its own raw silk. Legend has it that the person responsible for revealing the secret of silk was a Chinese princess. In leaving her homeland to marry a foreign prince, it was said, she smuggled some silkworms and mulberry leaves with her, along with the secret for how to weave silk. Why did she do this? According to legend, she wanted to be sure she would always have lovely silk dresses to wear in her new home.

The Silk Road

Silk was so important a commodity that a major trade route was named for it—the Silk Road. This system of caravan tracts linked China with the West. Traders made their way back and forth on these roads, trading in silk and other goods. Camel caravans, similar to those involved in the salt trade, were common sights along the Silk Road.

Before there were sea routes connecting the East and the West, the Silk Road was the most important trade route between these two worlds. The 5,000-mile-long Silk Road began in China and wound its way around deserts and over mountains until it reached the shores of the Mediterranean. From there, goods were shipped across the sea.

The desire of the West for the silk of the East was of major importance in linking China to Europe. Ideas were exchanged, as well as goods. Over the centuries, however, the Silk Road became less and less safe. Bandits often preyed upon caravans, robbing them of their precious cargo. The Silk Road began to fall into disuse.

This picture from a map made in the Middle Ages shows a camel caravan traveling along the Silk Road.

In modern times, what was once a major trading route has become, in part, a highway between Pakistan and China. There is no more need for a Silk Road. After all, the silk-making process is no longer a secret. Silk farms, which raise silk worms in large numbers and spin their threads into cloth, flourish all over the world. New **synthetic** fibers exist that have replaced silk in certain types of clothing, such as stockings. Silk is no longer a precious commodity.

Gold, Eternal Symbol of Wealth

Throughout human history, gold has been a symbol of wealth and power:

- When the ancient Egyptians buried their kings in huge underground tombs, they filled the chambers with treasures that largely consisted of gold.
- The ancient Greeks celebrated it in myth—King Midas and his deadly golden touch, the golden fleece sought by Jason and his Argonauts.
- In the Middle Ages, European inventors vainly experimented, hoping to find a way to turn other metals into gold, the metal they prized most.
- Spanish *conquistadores*, or conquerors, invaded Mexico and Peru in the 1500s, searching for the mythical city of gold called El Dorado.

Gold is a soft yellow metal that is **malleable**. This means that it can be stretched and beaten into different shapes. The ancient Egyptians hammered it into thin sheets called leaves.

The Value of Gold

Gold possesses several qualities that have made it highly prized over the centuries. It has an attractive, distinctive color and luster. It is tremendously durable and nearly impossible to destroy. It does not tarnish or rust. It is soft and easy to shape, so it is ideal for making into jewelry or coins.

In addition to being prized for its qualities, gold is also difficult to acquire. Most of it is buried deep underground and is hard to reach. Only a small amount is pushed up near the surface by underground forces. When it is discovered in rocks, gold is always found mixed with other, less valuable, metals. Deposits of pure gold, known as lode deposits, are very rare.

The main sources of gold in the ancient world were nuggets found around rivers and streams. As underground rocks became exposed on the surface, running water ate away at them. Deposits of metals and minerals were washed away into streams. Soft gold forms into clumps called nuggets, unlike the smaller particles of harder metals. These streambed nuggets are known as placer deposits.

In ancient times, rich placer deposits of gold were found in China, India, Persia, and lands around the Aegean Sea. During the Middle Ages, the major sources of gold in Europe were in Saxony (northern Germany), Austria, and Spain.

Many current world governments keep reserves of gold in the form of bricklike bars called ingots.

The Rush for Gold

After Columbus claimed America for Spain, the flow of gold into Europe increased enormously. Most of it came from Central and South America. Mines under European control were excavated and worked, using slave labor. Temples filled with gold treasures were looted by Europeans. From 1492 to 1600, more than 225,000 kilograms of gold from South America were exported abroad. But this did not keep the world from wanting more.

The second great golden era dawned with the discovery of gold at Sutter's Mill in California in 1848. Tens of thousands of prospectors, hoping to strike it rich, descended on the little settlement between Sacramento, California, and Carson City, Nevada. Although a few lucky souls were able to find enough gold to make them rich, it was primarily merchants who got wealthy as the population of California mushroomed. By 1850, two years after the Gold Rush began, California had grown so much that it applied for statehood.

Gold prospectors place a load of dirt in a container, pour in lots of water, and swirl the dirt around. They are hoping to wash away everything but some gold nuggets.

A third "golden era" occurred between 1890 and 1915, with the discoveries of gold in Alaska, the Yukon (Canada), and South Africa.

Gold continues to be a precious commodity today. It is crafted into expensive jewelry. It is used in many electrical and electronic devices, including televisions and computers. Thin gold coatings on the surfaces of spacecraft and office windows have a cooling effect because they reflect the infrared rays of the sun.

California became a state on September 9, 1850.

Diamonds, Dazzling and Durable

Diamonds are the crystallized form of pure carbon. You may have heard human beings described as "carbon-based life forms." Carbon is indeed the basis of all living things and can be found in combination with other elements in all plants and animals.

A diamond is carbon in its most concentrated form. It is the hardest substance known. Not surprisingly, the word for this unique crystal is derived from a Greek adjective, *adamas*. The ancient Greeks used this adjective to describe anything that was so hard, it could not be destroyed.

A chemically pure diamond is colorless. The addition of any other elements adds color, such as yellow from nitrogen or blue from boron.

The Value of Diamonds

Diamonds are extremely rare and difficult to find. The conditions for their formation—intense pressure and heat—only occur deep within Earth. Diamonds began to form over a billion years ago, more than 90 miles under continents and some 125 miles under the ocean floor. Some reach the surface in **molten** rock that is forced up through breaks in rocks. Some become trapped near the surface. The first diamonds, like gold, were probably found in streambed deposits. Mines later became the primary source.

Their rarity is not the only thing that makes diamonds so precious, however. They are also highly prized for their bright, flashing beauty. To achieve this beauty, a "diamond in the rough" must go through a long and involved process. Diamonds mined from the earth must be sorted by hand on the basis of size, quality, shape, and color.

After sorting, a diamond must be skillfully cut and polished to produce the flashing stone that is so highly prized. As the hardest of all substances, a diamond can only be cut by another diamond. It is generally believed that the art of diamond cutting in Europe arose in Venice sometime after 1330, with diamond cutters using iron wheels coated with diamond dust. These days, diamond saws are used.

The Diamond Trade

For about a thousand years, beginning around the fourth century B.C., diamonds were only mined in India. No one knows exactly when diamonds first appeared in the West. The earliest mention of these gems is in Roman writing from around A.D. 100.

By the mid-1300s, Venice had become the diamond-trading capital in Europe. In the early days of European diamond trade, these precious gems were reserved for royalty. By the 1600s, wealthy members of the aristocracy were wearing them as well.

India continued to be the sole source of diamonds until 1725, when diamonds were discovered in Brazil. In the 1870s, major finds in South Africa created a dramatic increase in the production of diamonds. Today, the major producers are Australia, Russia, South Africa, Botswana, and Congo Republic.

About 80 percent of the world diamond trade is overseen by a single organization, the Central Selling Organization. It strictly controls the quantity and quality of diamonds on the market. In short, it ensures that diamonds continue to be a precious commodity.

Oil, a Precious Natural Resource

These days, the news is filled with talk of rising oil prices and fears that the world will run out of oil.

Often called "black gold," oil formed long ago when prehistoric organisms and **microorganisms** died and drifted down to the ocean floor. They were buried under sand and then subjected to pressure and heat. Subsequent chemical changes led to the formation of crude, or unrefined, oil. The pressure of Earth forced it upward into less dense rock until the oil was stopped by rock that it could not penetrate.

The oil stayed where it was for thousands of centuries, soaking into the rock like water into a sponge. Occasionally, some seeped to the surface.

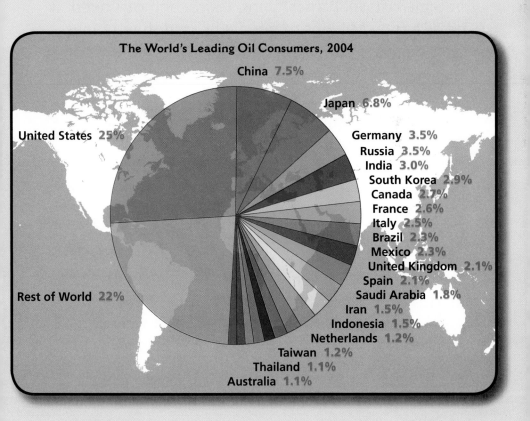

The World's Leading Oil Consumers, 2004

China 7.5%
Japan 6.8%
United States 25%
Germany 3.5%
Russia 3.5%
India 3.0%
South Korea 2.9%
Canada 2.7%
France 2.6%
Italy 2.5%
Brazil 2.3%
Mexico 2.3%
United Kingdom 2.1%
Spain 2.1%
Saudi Arabia 1.8%
Iran 1.5%
Indonesia 1.5%
Netherlands 1.2%
Rest of World 22%
Taiwan 1.2%
Thailand 1.1%
Australia 1.1%

The Value of Oil

Ancient people collected oil from large seeps. They used the heavy fluid to dress wounds and, finding that oil was flammable, in their lamps. It was not a precious commodity back then.

It wasn't until the twentieth century that the use of oil really became widespread. Petroleum, refined into gasoline, was found to be the best fuel to use in the popular new invention—the automobile. The increasing demand led to improved techniques for extracting oil. By the beginning of the twentieth century, oil fields were in operation in fourteen states as well as in Europe and the Far East.

As the century progressed, the need for oil became critical. Planes, ships, trains, and cars needed oil as a fuel. Millions of people heated their homes with oil. Now, we simply can't live without it.

The Oil Trade

Since oil drilling began in 1859, roughly 50,000 oil fields have been located. Over 90 percent of them have little effect on the world production of oil. Only two types of oil fields are truly significant: supergiants and world-class giants. Fewer than forty supergiants have been found worldwide, representing about half of the oil discovered thus far. Twenty-six of them are in the Persian Gulf. The oil-rich countries in this region include Kuwait, Saudi Arabia, Iran, and Iraq.

Sometimes the demand for oil has led to war. In 1990, Saddam Hussein, then leader of Iraq, ordered his army to invade neighboring Kuwait, hoping to take control of its vast oil fields. The United States successfully reclaimed the fields for Kuwait in a war known as the Gulf War.

Experts keep reminding us that it is only a matter of time before we run out of oil altogether. Some believe it will be within the next hundred years. The fact is, oil may be the most precious commodity of all!

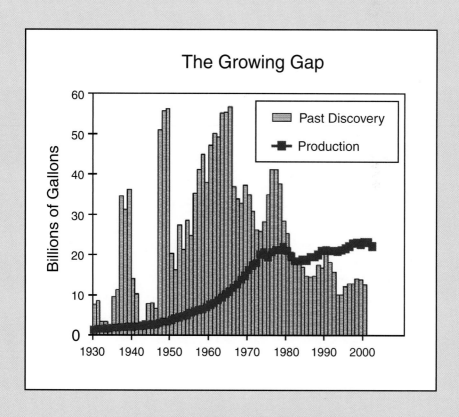

Now Try This

Create a Precious Goods Board Game

Divide up into small groups. Each group's job is to create a board game. The spaces on the game board will be labeled with the names of cities along a trade route. The game boards can then be traded and the game played by other groups.

Advance across a trade route by answering questions about precious goods you have read about.

1. One or two group members use books or the Internet to identify ten cities along the route of your choice.
2. Other group members label the spaces with city names and illustrate the board with drawings of precious goods.
3. Artistic members may design two game pieces, such as camels or traders.
4. Based on the facts in the book, have each person in your group write questions about a different commodity: salt, gold, silk, diamonds, or oil. Each group should write a total of 10 questions. Write the questions on one side of an index card. Write the answers on the opposite side.
5. Trade games with another group and take turns playing in groups of three. Have one person read the questions. Have the other two players take turns answering the questions. If the answer is correct, the player moves his or her game piece to the next city along the trade route. If the answer is incorrect, the player moves back a space. The first player to reach the end of the trade route is the winner.

Glossary

commodities *n.* any things that are bought and sold.

excavating *v.* exposing or uncovering by digging out, as a mine.

luster *n.* soft reflected light; sheen.

malleable *adj.* able to be shaped or formed as by hammering or pressure.

microorganisms *n.* organisms so small that they can only be seen with a microscope, such as bacteria.

molten *adj.* made liquid by heat; melted.

preserve *v.* to prevent something, such as food, from decaying or spoiling.

synthetic *adj.* created by humans rather than found in nature; artificial.